55 Ohio Waterfall Challenge Hikes

By Tina Karle

55 Ohio Waterfall Challenge Hikes
Lulu
North Carolina, USA

Please contact the author if a copy is wished for purchase: trinity091319@hotmail.com
Printed in the United States of America

ISBN: 978-1-387-73000-1

Imprint: Lulu.com 9 781387 730001

Front Cover: Ludlow Falls

By Tina Karle

Table of Contents

55 Ohio Waterfall Challenge Hikes

By Tina Karle

Acknowledgements

I would like to give thanks to GOD for giving us these beautiful falls to enjoy. Also, special thanks to my husband for all his patience in the many hours of driving and all the hiking involved in finding these amazing waterfalls. I also want to give thanks to John Haywood a fellow author in New York. He created 3 unique challenge hiking books for New York. Asked his permission about creating one for Ohio. He didn't mind at all! Look for his Challenge books on Amazon!

Disclaimer

This book is written to the best of the author's knowledge of known waterfalls. There ARE more waterfalls to be seen around Ohio! The author disclaims any liability from any accidents occurring while using this book as a guide. Most all trails listed in this book are safe to traverse. Take heed of certain trail conditions as they can change drastically from unknown weather conditions and you are cautioned to not place undue acceptance of all knowledge in this book and to use this guide at your own risk!

Excerpt from the Author

Do you know my friend? I would like to introduce you to someone who is dear to me! But first, I know, right? A hiking book, an odd place to put something like this. But this is a subject that I felt was important to share with you the reader. I want you to meet my friend Jesus. Now before the eye rolling starts and the stutters and curses start to flow, I'd like you to hear me out. For not many seem to know my Jesus. Yes, it is the same one that was born in a lowly manger to a virgin daughter of Abraham. Mary was her name. By her obedience to Father God in accepting a huge challenge, her simple acquiescence to be the hand maid of the Lord rocked this world. It brought forth our savior. What? Don't believe that a child was born without a father to do the act? Ah but that is where miracles begin my friend. For Jesus' birth was a miracle. His birth caused a king to slaughter thousands of innocent infants from a devil's rage to stop God's plan from happening. But God was with him. He survived and grew. Was tempted like we are and yet was without sin. They tortured and hung him on a cross; a common criminal if you please. But, on that wondrous third day he rose again in fulfillment of what He said would come to pass. It was written that that would happen in several places in the bible. Ah yes that book, that one that has been sitting on a shelf somewhere. Little used and dusty. It's in there though. That book, it is Jesus' for He is the Word, part of the Trinity. He came to earth to be a man. To become human to share in our pain and daily sufferings. He became man to understand us better, to know and understand our feelings and what we go through. Think he's just a myth, a fairy tale? Not important anymore? Well here is where I beg to differ. I know some of you will not share my views and will probably slander what I am saying here but I must share my thoughts. Read on if you are still curious to know the person whom I cannot live without

. For you see, Jesus is the friend I've always wanted. He longs to have a relationship with everyone, not just me. I met him one day you see quite by accident and it changed my life. He can and will change yours if you let Him. I really wasn't looking for Him but He was looking for me. He got my attention in very subtle ways. Oh, I thought I knew Him, having been brought up catholic. I read the children's stories, heard the Easter story and seen the movies. But that was face value stuff. That doesn't really show you who Jesus really is. Some may think so but I'm here to tell you it's not. Having known about Jesus all my life I thought I knew about him but I came to find out one evening, I didn't know him at all. For you see I was content in my life in how I was living and all I was doing at the time. But that was when God got my attention. He had a plan for me you see, just as He does for each of you. It was time I guess I woke up to the plan He had for me in my life. So, He slowly and subtly got my attention in little ways. An accident to me at work, meant to harm me came out to be used for God's good plan. In my convalescence doing light duty work God came and got my attention. It had happened before you see and I paid it a small mind but that night walking down that hallway to the lady's room, God woke me up to who He is. For He gave me a jolt you see something hard to explain with mere words. But from that moment on my life changed. From that moment life sped up for me, even though it was still the same day to day grunge, events started happening. A job change, my marriage put back to rights, relationships with friends changed, and time when I didn't have hardly a friend left, I met Jesus. Working at the IRS came the opportunity to listen to music and books on tapes. I stumbled across a person who knows my Jesus. I listened to his funny stories about life and how he was slowly introducing me to a Jesus I didn't know. But I wanted to know better! Jesse Duplantis changed my thoughts on what I thought I knew about Jesus. So, deciding to go back to church with my husband, I committed myself one evening to surrendering to accept Jesus into my life. From that moment on my life changed. Staying in church and learning who I really was helped to mold me into who I am today.

Oh, I'm guilty of leaving my home church for two years and going to a lesser church. But in those two years God used me and molded me and made me hunger for more of what I didn't understand. Going back to my church where I was saved helped turn me in the right direction. For you see it is all a choice. I myself can't make you accept Jesus. That is for you to decide yourself. I am just a messenger come to share what He's done for me. Although in church you receive do's and don'ts about how to live and what you should and shouldn't do once you are a Christian. These are important for boosting your faith. To some that is a drag. But it will help mold you to what Jesus says in His Word. My Jesus you can learn about that way to an extent which is good too, but it's the personal relationship I'm wanting to impart to you. That is something not often taught in church. For God wants to know us on a personal level. How you are wondering? Let me share with you how to know God and Jesus in a way He wants to be known. Hence why I am writing all this so-called boring stuff to you. Did you realize it is a simple matter? People make it hard all the time when the matter is very simple, for it is simple you

By Tina Karle

see! Most have put Jesus in a box. Not knowing that's what they've done. They take Him out on Sunday and put Him back again that night to maybe think about Him some during the week. Harsh? Maybe, but with many that is truth. They don't want Him interfering in "their" life. Not knowing that Jesus is a gentleman, He won't interfere. He will stand aside and let them do their own thing. Till they mess up and then want to pull him out of that box with their cry for help. He wants to share with you your everyday things, did you know that?

He wants you to talk with him about your problems, your relationship issues that are stagnant, your loneliness in not having a friend, or in your marriage issues. He wants to share in your triumphs and hold you when you're sad. He's there to pick you up when you're down and have you lean on Him when you can't fight no more. That's when He wants you to give it all to Him so He can fight for you. He's all around His very presence in the smallest things. Hard to believe but that's the power He has. From being creator of this our world yet humble and powerful enough to live inside of us. That itself is a mystery one in which I myself can't explain but simply accept. Ah but I digress. This book is meant to show you Jesus and God in a different way if you will allow Him too. For in this book you will see His handiwork everywhere. He made all those wonderful things for us to enjoy. I have put it into book form for you to get a glimpse of the power and majesty He brought for us to enjoy. For I believe waterfalls and the knowledge about them is a calling He has given to me to share with you the reader to enjoy. In creating this book while walking the woods, He was there beside me every step of the way, guiding me to the next set of falls. How did I find these falls you ask? I give all the glory to God and Jesus. For all I simply did was use topography maps and ask Jesus to come with me for the day. To guide me to the falls He wanted people to see. Whatever is hidden will be made known to those who wish to see. His gentle guidance in things not often seen right in front of us is why this book came to be. Same with all my other books. Things we take for granted and no longer see. Same with Jesus. Taken for granted, not really seen for who He really is. Let this book be a guide to show you a little bit of Him. Ask Him to go for a walk with you in the woods that are listed here in this book. Talk to Him while on that walk. Like you would a good friend. Don't think yourself crazy talking out loud to no one for He will be there walking beside you rejoicing that you chose to acknowledge Him. You may not physically with your ear hear His comment to you, but He will reveal Himself in many ways. A lovely bird song, a deer stepping out of the woods near you, a lone beautiful flower all speaks of His nearness to you. The rustle of the wind in the trees or the scent laden breeze tickling your face, all speak of His presence to woo you to Him. Will you let him woo you? As He did me? He's right there, always a gentleman, waiting to take your hand and walk that sunny path called life. It may contain clouds and some dreary days and may perhaps lead down into a dark hollow but hold tight to His hand and He'll lead you back to that sunny bright path leading to that waterfall tripping and skipping along. A voice you may hear in the chattering of the water may just be what you need to hear. So, let this book be that guide to hear His voice in a way you've not heard before….

If you would like to invite Jesus into your heart to be with you always simply say these words to start on a new path for a better and richer life…

As you say these words, if you'll believe them with your heart, you will be born again (Romans 10:9-10)

Jesus, come into my life. Forgive me of all my sins. I ask you to cleanse my heart, and make me a new person in You right now. I believe that You are the Son of God and that You died on the cross for me.

Jesus, I want to thank you for loving me enough to die for me. I accept all that Your shed blood bought for me on the cross, and I receive You as my Savior and Lord. In Your name, I pray. Amen.

If you just prayed this prayer, congratulations! You are a "new creature" in Christ and as 2 Corinthians 5:17 says, ". old things are passed away; behold, all things are become new." All of Heaven is celebrating! You have a brand-new life with Jesus and a bright future filled with faith and hope.

Forward

Waterfall- a fall or perpendicular descent of a stream of water. Thus, does Webster's Dictionary give the definition. In this book, you will find each waterfall with its official name and or unofficial name that's been given to name the falls. All names have come from the park they reside in, topographical maps, stream names, or if nothing else is reliable the name of the street the falls are on. Or in oft chances the author has come up with her own name for the waterfall! The waterfalls found in Ohio come in a variety of shapes and sizes. From the smallest step in the stream to the largest plunge found in Ohio, from the thinnest trickle of water to a raging torrent, viewing these falls can be a pleasure to be had.
Ohio's waterfalls come in many shapes and appearances. Each picture listed below will show a sample of the types of waterfall forms that are found in Ohio with their explanation of each.

One of the more familiar types is the **plunge or drop** waterfall. This is where a plume of water falls freely through the air before striking the base of the rock below.

Ramp waterfall. This is where water slides down a steeply inclined rock face without ever losing contact with the rock surface

Similar to the ramp is the **cascade waterfall.** This is a common waterfall found in Ohio. Water descends over the rock in many breaks, leaps and small tiers.

Fan Waterfall Waterfalls in this category are quite similar to that of the Horsetail variety. They share the common characteristic in that the waterfall drops and slides along a steep slope while consistently maintaining contact with the underlying cliff. However, the difference is that the shape of the waterfall is such that it looks more like a fan facing upside down.

Tiered This category of waterfalls describes waterfalls that have more than one vertical leap or tier to it from the perspective of a singular vantage point

Segmented This category of waterfalls involves the descending watercourse splitting up into two or more parallel segments or threads. Usually the cause of the split is some protruding rock in the middle of the watercourse before or during the course of the waterfalling cascade.

These are just a general listing of some of the types of waterfalls to be found around Ohio. Some waterfalls make up more than one of the above listed types. In this book, you will find many unique characteristics to the waterfalls. Each set of falls is unique to its own self and many change colors as the season's progress. From summer's deep, green colors and waters muted flow, to fall with colorful swirling leaves that eddy and swirl in the churning waters or being plastered flat to the moist rock surface, they add an enchanting rainbow of color to the falls. Ah but come winter part of the water stops and stands still for a little while and you can see the pale greens and arctic blue's in the face of the frozen falls. Springs thaw brings rampaging muddy waters with hues of a brilliant green surrounding the murky waters. Waterfalls, they each have their own personality to enjoy. So, come out and visit these marvelous wonders that God has created for all of us to enjoy.

Authors note:

I would like to interject a note here about these waterfalls. These waterfalls are for all to enjoy. PLEASE show common courtesy by picking up after yourself when visiting these places. Please don't leave boo loves who on the rocks, or trees write it in the dirt snap a picture and move on! As the saying goes along most trails pack in pack out what you bring. Take only pictures leave only footsteps. If all would keep their trash with them when they leave such places this will help preserve these special places for all to enjoy down the road.

By Tina Karle

About the Challenge

This book was written to be a challenge for those who love waterfalls, want to see something out of the way and not so crowded, but yet a unique and rewarding hike to something different. This book does NOT contain any GPS coordinates, directions to the waterfalls, or concise trail descriptions. This is where the challenge comes in. YOU become the detective to search out and figure out exactly where this waterfall is at and locating a trail if there is one. A true waterfall junkie's find and seek wrapped up in a book!

In this book you WILL have pictures of what the waterfall looks like. Trail clues to help guide you on the right path. A city, town, or village the falls is closest too. Some of these will be easy. Anything mentioned in quotation marks are a major clue! Some are not so easy.
I wrote this book so that you will get out there and visit the lesser-known falls and to avoid the summer time crowds that frequent the more popular spots located all around Ohio.

I have created a group on Facebook for you to go to and post your pictures as you do each hike. I DO ask that you don't share locations as that will spoil it for other hunters doing their own explorations. One thing I do ask of you is to post at least 5 selfies to show on the group of at least 5 of the regular falls and 1 if you figure the clues out, of the harder challenge hike given.

Those who complete and FIND all 5 of the harder challenge falls located at the end of the table of contents page will be rewarded with having one of the pictures shared as the wallpaper for a few weeks on the Facebook group.

This book is meant to be fun and a way to challenge oneself to get out there and find that waterfall with no added help from outside sources. Just you and your map/topo map/compass and a willingness to find that falls the old-fashioned way. Without outside help or everything being handed step by step. This book is written for that purpose. To get out there and enjoy nature and have fun finding the waterfall the way explorers of old once did.

Yes, the pictures are in black and white. It is extremely expensive to print in color. I apologize. You CAN on the group ask for additional hints if you are struggling with a particular waterfall, you are really wanting to see. I'll happily give out more clues to help you along the way if you need them. But again, this book is written to NOT hand out the falls easily. Some you may already have seen; others will be new and hopefully it will bring out your inner explorer to want to find this falls without much electronic help!

Also while in a certain area, check All trails, google maps or have one of my other hiking books handy to see other waterfalls that are located nearby to complete your day!

So put on those water boots/gym shoes/hiking boots, grab that most important water bottle and grab your camera or cell phone to grab those pictures! So you can show bragging rights on the group page that you are well on your way to finding all that Ohio has to offer in the way of quieter less known about; but just as beautiful waterfalls that don't get the attention the more popular one's receive!

Happy Hiking and exploring!

The Facebook group name to get hints, share your pictures is called: Waterfall Challenges of Ohio
There are questions to answer before joining said group. You will need this book to answer the first question!

FYI: ONE of the map numbers is wrong....can you figure out which one it is??

Hiking Key Page

The keys listed on this page are a guide to help you understand the terminology used in this book under the descriptions of the hikes and falls themselves.

Form:

Drop/Plunge: Descends straight down, has no contact with the rock

Cascade: Small falls made up of a large near vertical drop of water hitting the rocks continuously in a stair step fashion.

Tiered: A large waterfall that is broken up into 2 or more separate falls that is seen from one vantage point.

Ramp: This is where water slides down a steeply inclined rock face without ever losing contact with the rock surface

Fan: Waterfalls in this category are quite similar to that of the Horsetail variety. They share the common characteristic in that the waterfall drops and slides along a steep slope while consistently maintaining contact with the underlying cliff. However, the difference is that the shape of the waterfall is such that it looks more like a fan facing upside down.

Segmented: This category of waterfalls involves the descending watercourse splitting up into two or more parallel segments or threads. Usually the cause of the split is some protruding rock in the middle of the watercourse before or during the course of the waterfalling cascade.

Access:

This is the rating for the hike based on how much stamina/energy is required to walk the hike.

Easy: Simple to walk, not much effort required. Trail is generally flat with few hills.

Moderate: Some steep inclines or hills to be hiked as well as possible steps. You can become winded and may need an occasional rest. Some off-trail hiking is possible as well.

Hard: You will have a work out! Steep hills, sometimes no trail, general bushwhacking through high weeds, low level of tree and rock bouldering, sometimes trail is the creek itself leading to the falls and water shoes/boots are required. Rest breaks will be a must!

Height:

Most all the taller waterfalls have been measured for better accuracy on the true height of the falls. Medium to small falls have estimated heights.

Water:

Stream flow at a waterfall is determined by two factors: size of the watershed and recent precipitation history. A watershed is defined as the area whose runoff can flow to a given location. The larger the watershed the longer time of water flows. In smaller watershed areas to see the falls run, attention must be given to weather conditions. These are best seen right after a rain in general. Definitions for the seasons are provided below.

Spring: Weather is generally still cool. Rainy conditions, flowers and new greenery, melting snow, provides better water flow.

Summer: Generally hot and humid, less water flow, weeds are more promin ate, some falls are harder to see due to deeper green foliage. Snakes are more active.

Fall: Temperature is moderate to cool at night, low water flow is not uncommon, foliage becomes a brilliant background of bright colors.

Winter: Cold temperatures and less daylight, during colder temps low water flow can produce beautiful ice formations. Moderate flows are possible as well due to snow melt or rainfall. Trees are a dull brown in color, no foliage is visible, falls are easier to spot.

Year: Water has a year-round flow. Large creeks, rivers, and springs tend to run year round.

Distance:

Estimated distance from vehicle to the best view of the falls. Some of the hikes only have the city listed. For example, Overlook Falls has West Milton as the directions. Hikes that have only the city mentioned are harder hikes, have no trails, require a lot of wisdom, and usually are steep rough hikes that require a lot of climbing or scrambling over fallen objects. These are just GPS only hikes for that reason. Generally, are not for an afternoon stroll through the park type of hike!

Stream

Any given name from topography, or general maps labeled to a body of water, creek, stream, lake, or pond.

Restrooms:

This is for either a public bathroom, or Porto let or similar type restrooms.

Before You Begin Your Hike

1. Make sure you are wearing sturdy walking shoes. In some area's wearing waterproof boots/shoes are best for traversing through the creeks.
2. Wear comfortable clothing. Wear layers during winter months and remove as needed. Cotton is great to wear during summer months, as it will keep you cooler. Wool or Gortex is great for winter months. Don't forget your umbrella or rain jacket in case of a sudden storm. Watch the weather. Bring along an extra pair of socks or shoes in case of slippery trails, or a sudden tumble. Always, bring along an extra set of clothing when seeing waterfalls. A tumble can take one by surprise and can make for a miserable rest of your day if you have no other clothing with you!
3. Bring with you fluids to drink along your hike, if you plan to be out all day. A backpack is handy to have for carrying water and snacks as well as that handy extra pair of socks or gloves! Don't forget to bring along a snack for along the way to keep up your energy on the longer hikes!
4. Have with you or in your car some band aides, paper towels, washcloth, first aid kit, insect repellant, itch cream, and some aspirin for just such emergencies. The author carries with her a roll of toilet paper as well, for such certain emergencies that can't just wait!
5. Carry with you on your hike, if you so choose, your phone, a handy compass, food, water, map, umbrella, knapsack that can hold such items as well as a knife, hat, bandanna, GPS unit, and dry clothing. But this is up to each individual as to what they wish to carry.
6. To print out a handy topography or street map of the selected hike get on googlemaps.com, topozone.com, topomaker.com, and or mapquest.com. This will help you have an idea of where certain roads or creeks are located on the hike. The GPS coordinates are listed for almost every hike except otherwise noted.
7. Try not to hike alone if possible. If one decides to head out to see some of these beautiful falls, let a spouse, friend, family member know where you are going for safety reasons!
8. Hazards are REAL at waterfalls. And I urge you to be careful. So, I will write here of the basics of waterfall safety:

A. Watch where you walk. A root, or rock can send one tumbling if not careful. Algae covered rocks are also a bane to hikers as well, along with slick rock in some creeks. Even though the creek bottom is covered in water doesn't mean it isn't slippery, especially during summers dryer spells. Ice can also be dangerous especially if you don't know how thick it is, or how deep the water is beneath you.

B. The TOP of any waterfall can be the most dangerous spot of all. Use extreme caution when approaching any lip of a waterfall. That rock may not be as dry as one would expect and a tumble could be fatal if the falls are tall enough.

C. USE caution on any waterfall trail or no trail conditions. Wooden bridges can be slimy with moss, trails can turn mucky and muddy and be very slippery especially on a hill, watch one's footing even on dry dirt. Dry loose dirt can move and send you on a downhill careening ride if care isn't taken with one's footing! (author is speaking from experience this happening even in dry conditions!) Those loose sticks on the ground are not safe to tread upon as well as they can roll and cause you to lose your balance.

D. Watch children carefully around waterfalls. They should be under the supervision of a responsible adult.

E. Watch your pets if you should bring them with you. The same applies for them as for you on the trails.

F. Try NOT to hike alone, UNLESS you know the park or area very well. Even then have some sort of item for protection just in case!

9. Finally don't forget your camera, /tripod/phone/tablet to record for posterity your memorial visits to such beautiful places.
10. Please pick UP AFTER yourself at such beautiful places. Pack out what you packed into view said waterfalls. Please leave only footsteps and not decide to deface rock walls/trees/bridges or such places which ruins the view for others. Please try to show respect for the places you are visiting. Wouldn't it be nice to have it looking nice years from now so that your children's children will still have a place to come and enjoy what you yourself once enjoyed upon your visit?!

By Tina Karle

Ohio Map

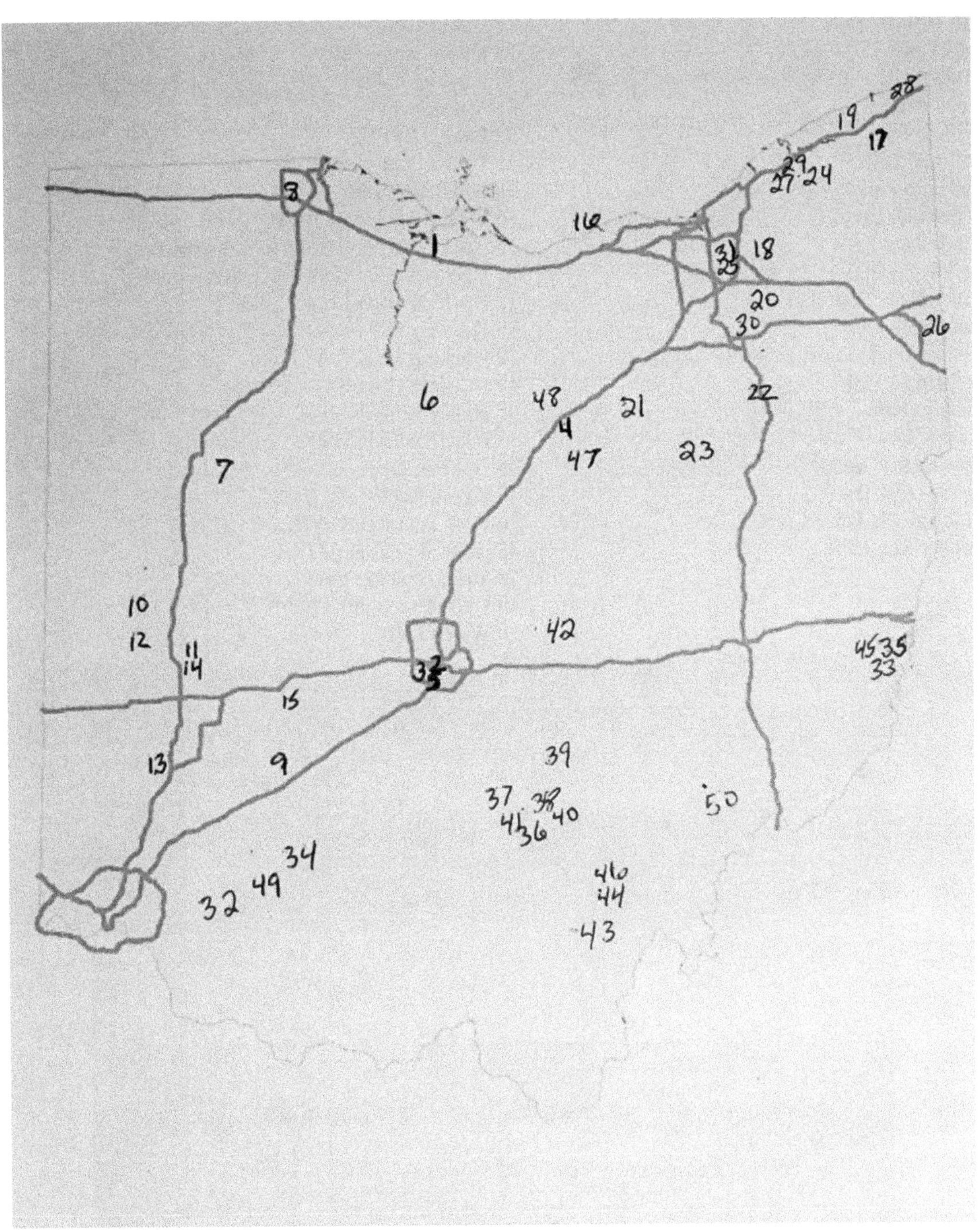

These are placed as close to where they are located as possible. They are NOT exact. The numbers correspond to the following list. The last five hikes in the book are not located on here for an additional challenge.

1 Cold Creek Falls
2 Emerald Falls
3 Indian Mound Reserve

55 Ohio Waterfall Challenge Hikes

4 Possum Run Falls
5 Quarry Trails Metro Park
6 Swift Hollow Falls
7 Walls Falls
8 Willow Falls
9 Armco Park
10 Ludlow Falls
11 Railroad Falls
12 Red barn Falls
13 Rentschler Forest
14 Sunderland Falls
15 Yellow Springs Creek Falls
16 Bay Village Waterfall
17Bear Creek Falls
18 Cascade Park
19 Cedarquist Park
20 Chagrin Falls
21 County Road Falls
22 Crown Hill Cemetery
23 Headwaters Trail
24 Hidden Falls-Paine Creek
25 Hooker Run Falls
26 Lake Hamilton Falls
27 Liberty Hollow Metro Park
28 Lulu Falls
29 Queen Anne Falls
30 Tip Top Falls
31 Whiskey Falls
32 Back Run Falls
33 Boord State Nature Preserve
34 Fallsville Falls
35 Forked Run State Park
36 Hocking Hills-Bison Hollow Preserve
37 Hocking Hills-Cantwell Cliffs Double Falls
38 Hocking Hills-Long Hollow
39 Hocking Hills-Rock Stahl's Nature Preserve
40 Hocking Hills-Rose Lake
41 Hocking Hills-Silver Falls
42 Honey Run
43 Lake Katherine Falls
44 Ophir & Opal Falls
45 Raven Rocks
46 Rock Run Road Falls
47 Route 423 Double Falls
48 Stone Chapel Falls
49 Unity Creek Falls
50 Welch Falls

By Tina Karle

North West Section

Cold Creek Falls

Height: 8 Feet	Restrooms: Yes
Water: Year	Distance: 200 Feet
Form: Drop	Access: Easy

Trail Hint
This one is for the parrot heads out there. Known as the original place before the singer came along. This waterfall offers a chance to kick back drink a few drinks, watch the fish jump the falls and enjoy a burger on the deck. You can boat or kayak up to the available dock close to this waterfall.

Location
Sandusky

By Tina Karle

Emerald Falls

Height: 10 Feet	Restrooms: No
Water: Spring/Winter	Distance: 300 Feet
Form: Cascade	Access: Easy

Trail Hint
The noise going on “above” this waterfall competes with the sound of the falls itself. The title gives away a very close location to where this waterfall is at. You might even Scioto a blue heron or two nearby….

Location
Dublin

Indian Run Falls

Height: 3/10/12 Feet	Restrooms: No
Water: Year	Distance: 200 Feet to 1000 Feet
Form: Drop/Cascade	Access: Easy

Trail Hint

Once home to the Wyandot Indians who used this area for fishing. Located close to a post office there are three sets of falls at this location. Popular in the summer, you will see kids swimming below the base of the falls. A street name will help give clues on how to locate this popular waterfall. There are trails here along with observation decks.

Location

Dublin

By Tina Karle

Possum Run Falls

Height: 10 Feet	Restrooms: No
Water: Spring/Winter	Distance: 1000 Feet
Form: Drop	Access: Moderate

Trail Hint
This waterfall you will need a left fork to decide how to go. A big store nearby is a place to park while you navigate traffic to find this falls. A salty good time is had by all when you pass by to enter the woods.

Location
Mansfield South

Quarry Trail Metro Park

Height: 20 Feet	Restrooms: Yes
Water: Spring/Winter	Distance: ¼ Mile
Form: Drop	Access: Easy

Trail Hint
You'll have an Irish time for sure at this once very large Quarry. Once known as Volkswagen Falls! Stone steps lead the way as you navigate steps built for mini giants. Condo's are becoming the norm here, where once there were rock trucks galore. Swimming is the norm in the pool of this falls come summer. Look for remnants that are left behind of the once little bug that took its final dive off the falls.

Location
Upper Arlington

By Tina Karle

Swift Hollow Falls

Height: 7 Feet	Restrooms: No
Water: Spring/Winter	Distance: 200 Feet
Form: Cascade	Access: Easy

Trail Hint
An orphanage once was on a farm located on a road with orphanage in the name. Many believe the old mansion nearby was the place where the orphanage was located at. But alas they would be wrong. A Joseph Swift owned the land where this falls resides. Tucked back make sure you aren't "gored" by the shape of the land. Watch the hump you must traverse and finding the creek will not leave you Vermillion.

Location
Henrietta

Walls Falls

Height: 8 Feet	Restrooms: No
Water: Year	Distance: 200 Feet
Form: Cascade	Access: Moderate

Trail Hint
A river runs under the road bridge. You will go "mad" trying to edit out the graffiti! There is a trail of sorts!

Location
Zanesfield

By Tina Karle

Willow Falls

Height: 8 Feet	Restrooms: No
Water: Spring/Winter	Distance: 300 Feet
Form: Cascade	Access: Moderate

Trail Hint
You'll have a Sandusky of a time walking the knobby rocks to see this waterfall. Look for a bridge where no "willows" reside.

Location
Tiffin

South West Ohio

By Tina Karle

Armco Park

Height: 5 Feet	Restrooms: Yes
Water: Spring/Winter	Distance: 200 Feet
Form: Cascade	Access: Easy

Trail Hint
Once known only to those who worked at AK Steel. Tennis anyone? Don't be a "turtle" about finding this easy to see waterfall! You might even have a Shaker good time getting to the base!

Location
Monroe

Ludlow Falls

Height: 15 Feet	Restrooms: No
Water: Year	Distance: 300 Feet
Form: Drop	Access: Easy

Trail Hint
A bridge over troubled waters. Also look for the fire station OR post office and don't get "fenced" in....

Location
Ludlow Falls

By Tina Karle

Railroad Falls

Height: 20 Feet	Restrooms: No
Water: Spring/Winter	Distance: ½ Mile
Form: Drop	Access: Moderate

Trail hint

Look for the tracks that are not live. You can start from where kings live. A weedy expanse awaits your trip on rails long dead. A creek bridge shows you the spot, but access must be taken behind. This be one hike never go alone if you are a female. Take a companion with you.

Location

Vandalia

Red Barn Falls

Height: 20 Feet	Restrooms: No
Water: Year	Distance: ¼ mile
Form: Cascade	Access: Moderate

Trail Hint
Do you smell that? A hill awaits those who choose to follow their nose down the incline. A walk will do you good but be sure to wear sturdy shoes. Are you good at climbing over trees to get to the prize? The old red barn gives away its hidden treasure.

Location
West Milton

By Tina Karle

Rentschler Forest

Height: 5 Feet	Restrooms: Yes
Water: Spring/Winter	Distance: 500 Feet
Form: Cascade	Access: Easy

Trail Hint
You will find remnants of the Miami Erie Canal in this area. You might even see a moon over "Miami" here as well! Don't let a summertime fee keep you away! You will get two for the price of one at this park! Listen for the sounds of water to guide you on the right path.

Location
Woodsdale

Sunderland Falls

Height: 20 Feet	Restrooms: No
Water: Spring/Winter	Distance: 100 Feet
Form: Drop	Access: Easy

Trail Hint
A street name gives away part of the location. You will have a rockin good time where you should park. The sound will lead you through a small nest of roots towards the sound of your prize. Rock climbing may be in your future if you wish to go to the base. Or a small dose of wet feet shouldn't put you ill at ease as you navigate the barrier for a view of the falls that is sure to please!

Location
Vandalia

Spring Late Spring Fall

By Tina Karle

Yellow Springs Creek Falls

Height: 7 Feet	Restrooms: No
Water: Year	Distance: 300 Feet
Form: Cascade	Access: Easy

Trail Hint
A busy road holds a secret path. The steps will lead the way. Community spirit abounds near this falls. But watch yourself lest the man in blue send you packing towards the cemetery!

Location
Yellow Springs

By Tina Karle

Bay Village Waterfall

Height: 20 Feet	Restrooms: No
Water: Spring/Winter	Distance: 300 Feet
Form: Cascade	Access: Easy

Trail Hint
Lake Erie calling your name? This park isn't located in "Columbia" South America! For a beachy good time find this pretty gem. Just make sure you don't "overlook" the view upstream! A swim will cool you off on a hot summers day! Stick around for the finale at the end of the day.

Location
Bay Village

Bear Creek Falls

Height: 15 Feet	Restrooms: No
Water: Spring/Winter	Distance: 100 Feet
Form: Cascade	Access: Moderate

Trail Hint
You might see a bear here, then again it might just be photographers bent over getting pictures! A guardrail protects this waterfall. A covered bridge will shelter you in case of a pop up rainstorm. Will you find the other secret waterfalls located here and a ¼ mile away? Do you Conneaut the way to find them? The Fox branch will lead you going south.
If you find all three post pictures to the group on Facebook!

Location
Kingsville

By Tina Karle

Cascade Park

Height: 10 Feet	Restrooms: Yes
Water: Spring/Winter	Distance: ½ Mile
Form: Drop	Access: Easy

Trail Hint
Don't let "Lynn" give you a "Case" of a gate closure! Will you park by the stinky or food smells? Will gravel get into your shoes? Left or right which will you choose? Four be the answer you are looking for! Some will run while others will be dry.

Location
Hudson

Cedarquist Park

Height: 30 Feet	Restrooms: Yes
Water: Spring/Winter	Distance: ¼ Mile
Form: Cascade	Access: Easy

Trail Hint
Let's play ball!! Can you find the hidden entrance into a secluded glen? A dirty path will show you the way. If she be running, you'll hear her faint sounds muted by the leaves that surround you up above. Winter will bring better sights of cliffs where none should be found.

Location
Ashtabula

By Tina Karle

Chagrin Falls

Height: 25 Feet	Restrooms: Yes
Water: Year	Distance: 200 Feet
Form: Cascade	Access: Easy

Trail Hint
Don't be "Chagrined" if you cannot find this. Don't be fooled by the dam in the park! Would you like popcorn or an ice cream to help cheer you up? Just watch those steps if your eye is on the cone you are holding! Is that the roar of traffic over a bridge or the sounds of a muted waterfall?

Location
Chagrin Falls

County Road Falls

Height: 15 Feet	Restrooms: No
Water: Spring/Winter	Distance: 250 Feet
Form: Drop	Access: Moderate

Trail Hint
The Mohican lies not too far away. Do you know Spanish? Tres, seis, ocho is the road you will need. At the left curve is where you would want to park. This one is located about a half mile from a T. You might not have to stray to far from your car to “hear” this waterfall!

Location
Brinkhaven

By Tina Karle

Crown Hill Cemetery

Height: 12 Feet	Restrooms: No
Water: Year	Distance: 200 Feet
Form: Drop	Access: Moderate

Trail Hint
Find the lake and follow north! A fencing master won't be required to locate this waterfall. Watch your step!

Location
Twinsburg

Headwaters Trail

Height: 8/15 Feet	Restrooms: No
Water: Spring/Winter	Distance: ¼-1/2 Mile
Form: Cascade/Drop	Access: Easy

Trail Hint
Built on the former Cleveland-Mahoning Railroad line. Head east once you find the trail. You won't need a Hanky or a "T-shirt Asbury" this spot is not hard to find! The second is labeled forty feet but I think fifteen feet from the trail is more like it!

Location
Mantua

By Tina Karle

Hidden Falls-Paine Creek

Height: 6/15 Feet	Restrooms: Yes
Water: Year	Distance: 1 Mile
Form: Cascade	Access: Moderate

Trail Hint
You will have a "hell" of a fun time navigating this twisty bendy creek. Where you start is where you do NOT want to end up when this life is over. Which way to go to find this hidden falls? Don't let Leroy or Thompson fool you with a petty small horseshoe. You want to keep striding south to gain the biggest prize of them all. Going south means going upstream? One note. Do NOT attempt to find this waterfall if the creek is flowing hard.

Location
Thompson

Hooker Run Falls

Height: 60 Feet	Restroom: No
Water: Spring/Winter	Distance: 500 Feet
Form: Bridal Veil	Access: Easy

Trail Hint
The stone house shows the way. Lots of "green" can be found here! Luckily there are no ladies of the night to be found here! Parking can be found where the Oaks knoll resides.

Location
Sagamore Hills

By Tina Karle

Lake Hamilton Falls

Height: 30 Feet	Restrooms: Yes
Water: Spring/Winter	Distance: 1 Mile round trip
Form: Cascade	Access: Moderate

Trail Hint
Are you too "yellow" to try this jaunt? Hope well keep you interested as you walk along the banks. Stay strong and continue to the end. Located in a city suburb creeking can be good fun as long as the yellow waters aren't raging!

Location
Struthers

Liberty Hollow Metro Park

Height: 25 Feet	Restrooms: Yes
Water: Spring/Winter	Distance: 1 Mile one way
Form: Cascade	Access: Moderate

Trail Hint
This falls is not where you think it resides. Are you ready for a slip and slide? How "Big" are your creek shoes? Is that the highway I hear? Which hollow do you choose? One leads no where and the other leads to a treasure. Going against the flow will help you find the inlet to this secret. Are you going to be too logged down to keep going? Avoiding the jams one might go up high and catch the scenic view.

Location
Painesville

By Tina Karle

Lulu Falls

Height: 10 Feet	Restrooms: No
Water: Spring/Winter	Distance: ¼ Mile
Form: Cascade	Access: Hard

Trail Hint
You will have a Lulu of a time finding her in this plot. Watch out for the grave diggers! You may have to hop and slide to get to the water. Walking against the flow will get you there in due course.

Location
Kingsville

Queen Anne Falls

Height: 60 Feet	Restrooms: Yes
Water: Spring/Winter	Distance: ¼ Mile
Form: Cascade	Access: Moderate

Trail Hint
Will you gain access to this waterfall with the "Queens" permission? Indians "point" the way off a road people go "Vrooman" along! Look for a bridge over a Grand view. The creek you are looking for will point you in the "right" way. Rock hopping as you head upstream can be slick or dry depending on time of year!

Location
Painesville

By Tina Karle

Tip Top Falls

Height: 10/15 Feet	Restrooms: No
Water: Spring/Winter	Distance: 300 Feet
Form: Tier	Access: Moderate

Trail Hint
You will have a “tip top” time enjoying a bite here. Stay for the food then search for the falls. Look for a guardrail to lead you to the top. Don’t let the dumpster throw you off! A spit of land shows you another surprise that’s across from a back door. Can you find the two different ways that lead to the base? One is a concrete slide the other is a rock climbers treat. If your brave and venture out on the cliff top, can you find the path into a cliffy den that sports a musical serenade? One note of caution the cliff and rocks can be slippery. Use wisdom near the top of the falls.

Location
Stow

Whiskey Falls

Height: 16 Feet	Restrooms: No
Water: Spring/Winter	Distance: ½ Mile
Form: Drop	Access: Hard

Trail Hint

Will the name of the falls give way to the hint on it's location? Parking could be an issue unless you have a "horse" to guide you! At the T you would think to go right but in reality, you must go left. Follow the "view" to the half moon out cropping. Can you sidestep down to the creek below? A fork appears in the creek. The left tine leads the way. Although if one has time there is a right tine to explore too. A "park view" at the right will be a lovely surprise. But it is the left I am showing for this challenge today. No whiskey jugs found but you'll have a rusty good time!

Location

Brecksville

By Tina Karle

South East Ohio

Back Run Falls

Height: 5 Feet	Restrooms: No
Water: Spring/Winter	Distance: ½ Mile
Form: Cascade	Access: Moderate

Trail Hint
You will have a "Foozer" of a time finding a place to park! You might even reach a dead end…Hark I hear the woods calling your name! Find the path and trail the creek. Just don't slip and slide or you'll wind up downstream on top of the falls!

Location
Hamlet

By Tina Karle

Boord State Nature Preserve

Height: 6 Feet	Restrooms: No
Water: Spring/Winter	Distance: 800 Feet
Form: Cascade	Access: Easy

Trail Hint
You will not be “boord” at this nature preserve! Eastern Hemlocks line the cliffs and verdant wildflowers appear come spring. Follow the blatant path that will lead you towards a wooden overlook. Parking can be had by searching for a falls run road.

Location
Cutler

Fallsville Falls

Height: 22 Feet	Restrooms: No
Water: Spring/Winter	Distance: ¼ Mile
Form: Cascade	Access: Moderate

Trail Hint
From "town" make sure to "Carey" your camera gear and wet shoes! A sign will point the way to where to park. After a rain you will be slip sliding along in the woods as the path goes up and down potholes. Spotted through the trees is a sparkling jewel. Fisherman delight to cast their lines. Stop to enjoy the view of this before heading on down the path. Multiple paths lead off towards the "clear" views. Which path will you take? Some are sure to send you sliding while another will meander gently down to the creek below. In late spring and summer watch walking as these rocks are quite slick.

Location
Hillsboro

By Tina Karle

Forked Run State Park

Height: 18 Feet	Restrooms: No
Water: Spring/Winter	Distance: 700 Feet
Form: Cascade	Access: Easy

Trail Hint
Down by the "Ohio" close to West Virginia along a "Scenic Hwy," you will come across an unusual term called "Long Bottom." A "Hollow" Road will lead you northward. Do you trust your "dam" GPS? Will it lead you to the right spot? If you've come to a "Little Forest" you've gone to far. Will you figure out how to park? Or will you want to "run" a "fork" through that GPS that's leading you astray?!

Location
Long Bottom

Hocking Hills-Bison Hollow Preserve

Height: 4/15 Feet	Restrooms: No
Water: Spring/Winter	Distance: 200 Feet
Form: Cascade	Access: Moderate

Trail Hint
To park here you must drive over a creek on a road that begins with 'School." Was sheep dipped at this waterfall? A tiny bit of rock climbing will have you facing a crack in the rocks. NO ATV'S please or you'll see the men in blue! To gain access to the base a creek hop and woods walk would be required. Please be respectful at this preserve. Pick up after yourself and be polite if anyone comes to chat.

Location
South Bloomingville

By Tina Karle

Hocking Hills-Cantwell Cliffs Double falls

Height: 12 Feet	Restrooms: No
Water: Spring/Winter	Distance: ¼ Mile
Form: Drop	Access: Easy

Trail Hint

To find me you must look past the obvious. Parking is in a bend in the road out of site of the normal parking abode. Be cautious when you go to park if you're on a tilt you might get stuck! Look past the locked gate to find the path that heads south east. I wouldn't try driving past that gate or an iron gate might hold your future. Do you see rocks? That form a bridge? Cross it if you please to see that your seeing double for your trouble. The base isn't to hard to ace, where beauty resounds her melodic sound. Do you see a dragon or a dog? If you so choose will you discover my ruse? There's more to see if you know which path or lack of path that turns you into a daredevil! How many can you find? Can four be an important number? Are you brave to try your luck? Where cliffs abound and sound lures you on. Just watch your steps for your treading where not many are found….

Location
Gibisonville

What you are looking for 1st   bonus finds a trick to find

Hocking Hills-Long Hollow

Height: 50 Feet	Restrooms: No
Water: Spring/Winter	Distance: ¾ Mile One Way
Form: Drop	Access: Moderate

Trail Hint

Don't "Pine" away for a parking spot. There is always bound to be one available if you arrive early enough! Don't let the dust choke you as climbers gather their gear to head off to hit the cliffs! I've heard tell that they once fit 21 horses in a cave along the way to this waterfall! How "LONG" is this hike? Will you see the hidden falls along the way? A double for your trouble set of falls awaits you at the end of this journey!

Location

South Bloomingville

By Tina Karle

Hocking Hills-Rock Stahl's Nature Preserve

Height: 20 Feet	Restrooms: No
Water: Spring/Winter	Distance: 1.5 Miles Round Trip
Form: Horsetail/segmented	Access: Moderate

Trail Hint

Which Rock Stull Road will you chose? You need to know you are going in the right direction! A dirt and gravel pull-off gives the clue on where to park. When you come to a fork in the path rights always seem to be the way to go. You will take "steps" in the right direction if you follow the correct path! Not one but two will you see if you found the end of the hollow. A photography hint: head right to the second horseshoe lil hollow and turn to face the falls. Focus your camera at an angle to catch both sets of falls as seen in picture below.

Location

Rock Bridge

Hocking Hills-Rose Lake

Height: 60 Feet	Restrooms: Yes
Water: Spring/Winter	Distance: 1 ½ Miles One Way
Form: Drop	Access: Moderate

Trail Hint
Do you have what it takes to find this set of falls? "Cedars" start your journey and carry you past "Whispering" Falls that abound along your journey. When you pass the very tall plume waterfall take a bend to the right, then a bend to the left then in a short while watch for the way to be made clear. Your trip will be made rosy if you find the right way! An arch resides back here too; are you clever enough to figure out it's rocky domain?

Location
South Bloomingville

By Tina Karle

Hocking Hills-Silver Falls

Height: 110 Feet	Restrooms: No
Water: Spring/Winter	Distance: ½ Mile One way
Form: Cascade	Access: Moderate

Trail Hint
"Parish" the thought of ever finding this falls! Do you know Grandma Gatewood? People thought she was a "Queer" old lady but she established a wonderful route to see amazing scenery! Don't let the big boulders by the creek keep you from finding the "hidden" prize. A hint to make this easier would be to look for the crossing near where you park! A gravel area off of the main route from South Bloomingville. You park before the route goes up the hill. You know your close to your prize if across the creek you hear a "whispering" cave close by. BUT if you see that cave you've gone to far!

Location
South Bloomingville

Honey Run

Height: 10 Feet	Restrooms: No
Water: Spring/Winter	Distance: 1000 Feet
Form: Cascade	Access: Easy

Trail Hint
"Austin" Powers would like this road! Kokosing along for the ride with him. "Honey" would be in the back seat. Driving along looking for a "sign" to park their vehicle. They discover a "caves" area for camping and wonder if Dr Evil is located near the river. Upon finding a trail they "bridge" the gap to find the clue amid the cliffs!

Location
Millwood

By Tina Karle

Lake Katherine Falls

Height: 10 Feet	Restrooms: No
Water: Spring/Winter	Distance: 1 Mile RT
Form: Cascade	Access: Easy

Trail Hint
Let the "beaver" lead the way to the road that has "Katherine" in it. Don't let the "dam" thing get in your way from getting to the falls! Let the woods be your guide. Watch crossing the span for your goal to be found!

Location
Jackson

Ophir & Opal Falls

Height: 15 Feet	Restrooms: No
Water: Spring/Winter	Distance: 2 Miles One Way
Form: Cascade	Access: Moderate

Trail Hint
Parking location: Trienta nueve dot uno uno siete uno cuatro comma negative ochenta y dos dot seis cuatro dos cuatro cuatro seis.
Don't be yellow if you cannot figure out the parking. Pass the gate and sometimes you have to go uphill to go downhill! When you get to the stream go with the flow! Don't let the small teaser fool you! Go down and round to view the sound. Then continue to go with the flow till you change your flow at the T. Upstream proves the wisest way to go. Follow to find Ophir and a smaller one that's just as dear!

Location
Jackson

By Tina Karle

Raven Rocks

Height: 15 Feet	Restrooms: No
Water: Spring/Winter	Distance: ¼ Mile
Form: Cascade/Drop	Access: Moderate

Trail Hint
Watch out for the "crumy" road. You will be "pining" for this creek! Take the trail and don't let the fat mans misery stop your "steps" from heading downstream. A trail blaze is required to see what the echoing sounds reveal! Continue to flow with the waters and at the juncture don't be "left" confused! Let the flow drive you along until a secret swale turns you leftwards. Find the treasure and call it a day!

Location
Wilson

Rock Run Road Falls

Height: 5/10 Feet	Restrooms: No
Water: Spring/Winter	Distance: 200 Feet
Form: Drop	Access: Easy

Trail Hint
Don't get too "salty" crossing this creek on a Rocky Road! "Lick" your wounds as you go right left right stop! Pull over to notice the cliff side retreat. I wouldn't venture far or you will flat out run out of rock!

Location
Jackson

By Tina Karle

Route 423 Double Falls

Height: 20 Feet	Restrooms: No
Water: Spring/Winter	Distance: 500 Feet
Form: Tier	Access: Moderate

Trail Hint
Make sure you don't trip over the "fox hole" as you look for the road needed to find this falls. This "township" area doesn't contain an original name for the road you seek. A walk in the "park" will be necessary to find this elusive treasure. OR, a walk heading north along a road might help spot the prize. Can you find the tricky way down to see these double for your trouble set of falls?

Location
Newcastle

Stone Chapel Falls

Height: 10 Feet	Restrooms: No
Water: Spring/Winter	Distance: 400 Feet
Form: Drop	Access: Moderate

Trail Hint
Going to the "chapel" on the "hill" and we're gonna get married! Watch for a "Trefz" gravel lay by for parking. Have the bride wear good foot wear or the "stones" and the stickers will reach out and snag that beautiful dress! Will you find the way? It's a perfect area for a wedding shoot if your bride can handle wet feet? And good balance to navigate the "roses" down the tricky slope! Hold on to your bride lest you SLIP and slide!

Location
West Union

By Tina Karle

Unity Creek Falls

Height: 10 Feet	Restrooms: No
Water: Spring/Winter	Distance: 200 Feet
Form: Drop	Access: Easy

Trail Hint
"White Oaks" dot the way on your journey to find this out of the way set of falls. You will find "Unity" with the homeowner as long as you don't do any fishing! Will you spot the chimney that "guards" the path to this waterfall? There's no place to park unless you pass a "guard" first. Crossing a large bridge takes you a step backwards on your hunt!

Location
Hamersville

Welch Falls

Height: 10/15 Feet	Restrooms: No
Water: Spring/Winter	Distance: 300 to 1000 Feet
Form: Drop	Access: Moderate

Trail Hint
"Laurel and Hocking" will give you a good run for your money. Don't go "speeding" along to fast or they might think you are off the wrong track! If your quick and make your escape over the river you just might find the Welch's jam singing to you from the ravine!

Location
Fillmore

By Tina Karle

Extra Hard Challenge Falls

Beach City Wildlife Area Waterfall

Height: 10 Feet	Restrooms: No
Water: Spring/Winter	Distance: ¼ Mile
Form: Drop	Access: Moderate

Trail Hint
Dundee is a beautiful waterfall but have you known about this set of falls? Do you hear a train? "Wilmot" you know where to look? Horses know the way but are stopped by boulders blocking the way. Don't turn "aside" to the left or you'll be bucked off your horse and take a dunking into the stream!

Location
Dundee

By Tina Karle

Contour Falls

Height: 50 Feet	Restrooms: No
Water: Spring/Winter	Distance: 1 Mile One Way
Form: Cascade	Access: Moderate

Trail Hint
To park you must park where trains stopped at the "station." Will you receive a "tow" along a path as you can hear the old refrain "Go North!" How long will you walk? One, Two, "Three" strikes you've found it! Now let the fun begin! You'll know your going right when logs and rocks abound in the creek to be found. Heading against the flow what's this? A fork in the creek? Only the "right" person will know the way to go. Will you find this waterfall and her other half hidden in a nook? They'll be no "cooking" at this falls that's blessed with two known names!

Location
Sagamore Hills

Diamond Falls

Height: 70 Feet	Restrooms: No
Water: Spring/Winter	Distance: 1 Mile One Way
Form: Drop	Access: Hard

Trail Hint
Don't let the "little beavers" knock you into the creek! Their gnawed trees that are down could send you sliding down the hill! Find the old bed that once was dominated by rail cars. Can you field the "rocky" blockade? Your treasure awaits along the cliffside IF she be running. Is that a sparkle I see? Will you find the lost diamond ring purposed to reside near the base of this falls? To park find "1038" and look for rocks that block a gravel edge. Space for a car resides if you know where to look!

Location
Fredericktown

By Tina Karle

Mustapha Island Falls

Height: 10 Feet	Restrooms: No
Water: Spring/Winter	Distance:200 Feet
Form: Drop	Access: Easy

Trail Hint
I think I "hear" West Virginia calling! The "Ohio" will easily flood this waterfall come spring! I think I hear the "river" calling will you "cave" into the pressure of finding this elusive set of falls? Or will you pass by the secret that a passerby might miss? I see a "stream" of water soaking the road in muddy car prints, is that a hint? Don't let the waterfall "bushes" throw you off!

Location
Torch

Rattlesnake Creek Falls

Height: 20 Feet	Restrooms: No
Water: Year	Distance: ¼ Mile
Form: Drop	Access: Moderate to Hard

Trail Hint
I hear those trains a running. Along a smooth and live track! How brave are you? Do you fear "heights?" Can you make it to the other side? A slide or a side step will be required to gain this ultimate swimmers delight. Where iron rungs are hammered into the rock as kids egg each other on to flip or jump. Fisherman dot the way to catch the fish when no ones around. I wouldn't attempt this after a storm. Currents are swift and down you'll drift To Paint Creek Lake!

Location
East Monroe

Index

By Tina Karle

About the Author

Tina Karle has a degree in Photography from New York Institute of Photography and over Twenty four years of in the field experience in landscape photography. She is the author of *Falling Waters of Ohio (109 Hikeable Falls in Ohio), Falling Waters of Ohio; a coffee table book, 200 Waterfall Hikes in Ohio, Celebration of Flowers, 120 Waterfall Hikes Around Cincinnati Ohio, 110 Waterfall Hikes Around Madison Indiana, 85 Waterfall Hikes of Dayton, 200 Waterfalls of Northeast Ohio, 55 Waterfall Hikes of Louisville Kentucky, 155 Waterfall Hikes of Kentucky, 300 Tristate Waterfalls of Ohio, Kentucky & Indiana, 200 Hikeable Waterfalls of Ohio(revised edition) and Tumbling Waters of Ohio(Coffee Table)* was born and raised in Ohio and grew up mostly in Kentucky. Her enjoyment of looking for new falls with her husband; has kept her on a continual journey throughout Ohio, Indiana, New York and now Kentucky. Using her professional photographers keen eyesight and with the help of God's good grace, for rain, she used her passion for waterfalls and put together books for all to enjoy. When not traveling around the states looking for waterfalls or flowers, she resides near Cincinnati, Ohio with her husband, three cats, and four parrots. Other hiking books will be coming out soon on Seneca and Cayuga Finger Lakes area New York Waterfalls, Grayson Lake Kentucky Waterfalls, revised Cincinnati Ohio Waterfall book, and Indiana Waterfall Hikes!

www.ingramcontent.com/pod-product-compliance
Ingram Content Group UK Ltd.
Pitfield, Milton Keynes, MK11 3LW, UK
UKHW051129260726
13967UKWH00010B/2937

9 781387 730001